SCORE
KAPLAN
Educational Centers

LEARNING ADVENTURES: QUIZ ME!

Grades 1–2

By the Staff of Score@Kaplan

Foreword by Alan Tripp

Simon & Schuster

This series is dedicated to our
Score@Kaplan parents and children—
thank you for making these books possible.

Published by
Kaplan Educational Centers and Simon & Schuster
1230 Avenue of the Americas
New York, NY 10020

Copyright © 1998 by Kaplan Educational Centers

Special thanks to: Elissa Grayer, Donna Mackay (Graphic Circle Inc.), Rebecca Geller Schwartz, Linda Lott, Janet Cassidy, Marlene Greil, Nancy McDonald, Sarah Jane Bryan, Chris Wilsdon, Janet Montal, Jeannette Sanderson, David Stienecker, Dan Greenberg, Kathy Wilmore, Dorrie Berkowitz, and Molly Walsh

Head Coach and General Manager, Score@Kaplan: Alan Tripp
President, Score@Kaplan: Robert L. Waldron
Series Content and Development: Mega-Books
Project Editor: Julie Schmidt
Production Coordinator: Jobim Rose
Managing Editor: Brent Gallenberger
Cover Design: Cheung Tai
Cover Photograph: Michael Britto

Manufactured in the United States of America
Published Simultaneously in Canada

January 1998
10 9 8 7 6 5 4 3 2 1

ISBN: 0-684-84824-4

Contents

Dear Parents,

Your child's success in school is important to you, and at Score@Kaplan we are always pleased when the kids who attend our educational centers do well on their report cards. But what we really want for our kids is not just good grades. We also want everything that good grades are supposed to represent:

- We want our kids to master the key communication systems that make civilization possible: language (spoken and written), math, the visual arts, and music.
- We want them to build their critical-thinking skills so they can understand, appreciate, and improve their world.
- We want them to continually increase their knowledge and to value learning as the key to a happy, successful life.
- We want them to always do their best, to persist when challenged, to be a force for good, and to help others whenever they can.

These are ambitious goals, but our children deserve no less. We at Score@Kaplan have already helped thousands of children across the country in our centers, and we hope this series of books for children in first through sixth grades will reach many more households.

Simple Principles

We owe the remarkable success of Score@Kaplan to a few simple principles. This book was developed with these principles in mind.

- We expect every child to succeed.
- We make it possible for every child to succeed.
- We reinforce every instance of success, no matter how small.

Assessing Your Child

To assess your child's skills, ask yourself the following questions.

- How much is my child reading? At what level of difficulty?
- Has my child mastered language skills like spelling, grammar, and syntax?
- Does my child have the ability to express appropriately complex thoughts when speaking or writing?
- Does my child demonstrate mastery of all age-appropriate math skills, such as mastery of addition and subtraction facts, multiplication tables, division rules, and so on?

These questions are a good starting place and may give you new insights into your child's academic situation.

What's Going on at School

Parents will always need to monitor the situation at school and take responsibility for their child's learning. You should find out what your child should be learning at each grade level and match that against what your child actually learns.

The quizzes in *Learning Adventures: Quiz Me! Grades 1–2* were developed using the standards developed by the professional teachers associations. As your child tackles the questions in *Learning Adventures: Quiz Me! Grades 1-2*, you might find that a particular concept hasn't been taught in school or hasn't yet been mastered by your child. This presents a great opportunity for both of you. Together you can learn something new.

Encouraging Your Child to Learn at Home

This book is full of fun questions you can do with your child to build understanding of key concepts in language arts, math, and science. The questions are designed for your child to answer independently. But that doesn't mean that you can't work on them together, or invite your child to share the work with you. As you help your child learn, please bear in mind the following observations drawn from experience in our centers:

- Positive reinforcement is the key. Try to maintain a ratio of at least five positive remarks to every negative one.
- All praise must be genuine. Try praises such as: "That was a good try" or "You got this part of it right."
- When a child gets stuck, giving the answer is often not the most efficient way to help. Ask open-ended questions, or rephrase the problem.
- Be patient and supportive. Children need to learn that hard work pays off.

There's More to Life Than Academic Learning

Most parents recognize that academic excellence is just one of the many things they would like to ensure for their children. At Score@Kaplan, we are committed to developing the whole child. These books are designed to emphasize academic skills and critical thinking, as well as provide an opportunity for positive reinforcement and encouragement from you, the parent.

We wish you a successful and rewarding experience as you and your child embark upon this learning adventure together.

Alan Tripp
General Manager

HOW TO USE THIS BOOK

The quizzes in this book will help you and your child locate possible problem areas or gaps in learning in language arts, math, and science. The questions cover a wide range of material that your child *might* have encountered in the first and second grades.

The *Learning Adventure* workbooks that Score@Kaplan publishes are a useful complement to these quizzes. There are four different workbooks for grades 1–2:

> *Learning Adventures: Math, Grades 1–2*
> *Learning Adventures: Reading, Grades 1–2*
> *Learning Adventures: Science, Grades 1–2*
> *Learning Adventures: Animals, Grades 1–2*

The fun activities in these workbooks will help your child practice and hone skills in particular subjects. Have your child take each quiz in this book *before* doing the activities in the corresponding workbook, to identify specific areas where she needs more practice. Or have her take the quizzes *after* doing the activities to check on how much she has learned.

The quizzes are not meant to serve as definitive tests of your child's intelligence or an indication of subject mastery. These quizzes will help you and your child spend more time on problem areas or unfamiliar material. Keep the focus on "serving the learning in welcome helpings"; never pressure your child to "score high" or "learn on command."

You can be sure that there is no *right* way for your child to take these quizzes. Take all the quizzes in a row, or take one quiz one day and save the others for different occasions. Your child can quiz himself—like taking a fun activity break—or you can help your child and work through the quizzes together. Just remember that the purpose of all Score activities is to make learning enjoyable!

Math

$2 + 2 + 3$

INTRODUCTION

As you and your child prepare to tackle the questions in this home learning quiz in math, remember that help is available if you need it. The specific skills tested in this quiz are covered in the companion publication *Learning Adventures: Math, Grades 1–2*, published by Score@Kaplan and Simon & Schuster. This richly illustrated workbook is full of fun activities that will teach your child all the skills he or she needs to master.

Have your child take each quiz *before* doing the activities in the corresponding workbook, to identify specific areas where she needs more practice. Or have her take the quizzes *after* doing the activities to check on how much she has learned.

Home Learning Quiz

See how many of these you can get right! Read carefully. Use scrap paper if you need to write anything down. Then fill in the answer bubble. Fill in the (e) bubble if you haven't been taught something in the question. Fill in the (f) bubble if you've learned this in school, but it's still hard for you.

1. **Which number is missing? 57, 58, _____, 60**

    (a)   56
    (b)   95
    (c)   59
    (d)   61
    (e)   We haven't studied this in school yet.
    (f)   We've studied this, but it's still hard for me.

                 (a) (b) (c) (d) (e) (f)

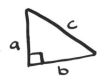

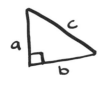

(5,7)

2.   **Which rabbit is in a circle?**

(a)   first
(b)   second
(c)   third
(d)   fourth
(e)   We haven't studied this in school yet.
(f)   We've studied this, but it's still hard for me.

3.   **Which number comes next? 5, 10, 15, 20, ___**

(a)   15
(b)   30
(c)   5
(d)   25
(e)   We haven't studied this in school yet.
(f)   We've studied this, but it's still hard for me.

4. Which number is even?

(a)   3

(b)   7

(c)   11

(d)   4

(e)   We haven't studied this in school yet.

(f)   We've studied this, but it's still hard for me.

ⓐ   ⓑ   ⓒ   ⓓ   ⓔ   ⓕ

5. Round off 489 to the closest hundred.

(a)   400

(b)   40

(c)   500

(d)   5000

(e)   We haven't studied this in school yet.

(f)   We've studied this, but it's still hard for me.

ⓐ   ⓑ   ⓒ   ⓓ   ⓔ   ⓕ

6. 12 − 9 = ____

(a)   9

(b)   3

(c)   12

(d)   4

(e)   We haven't studied this in school yet.

(f)   We've studied this, but it's still hard for me.

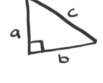

ⓐ   ⓑ   ⓒ   ⓓ   ⓔ   ⓕ

Quiz Me!

7. **3 + 4 + 2 = _____**

    (a) 7

    (b) 6

    (c) 10

    (d) 9

    (e) We haven't studied this in school yet.

    (f) We've studied this, but it's still hard for me.

8. **21 + 34 = _____**

    (a) 55

    (b) 56

    (c) 46

    (d) 37

    (e) We haven't studied this in school yet.

    (f) We've studied this, but it's still hard for me.

9. **48 − 25 = _____**

    (a) 26

    (b) 25

    (c) 23

    (d) 63

    (e) We haven't studied this in school yet.

    (f) We've studied this, but it's still hard for me.

10. **Which one helps you solve 14 − 8 = ____?**

    (a)   8 + 4 = 12
    (b)   4 + 4 = 8
    (c)   6 + 8 = 14
    (d)   14 − 4 = 10
    (e)   We haven't studied this in school yet.
    (f)   We've studied this, but it's still hard for me.

11. **Which helps you solve 4 × 2 = ____?**

    (a)   4 + 2 = 6
    (b)   2 + 4 = 6
    (c)   42
    (d)   2 + 2 + 2 + 2 = 8
    (e)   We haven't studied this in school yet.
    (f)   We've studied this, but it's still hard for me.

12. **27 + 34 = ____**

    (a)   53
    (b)   61
    (c)   51
    (d)   62
    (e)   We haven't studied this in school yet.
    (f)   We've studied this, but it's still hard for me.

13. $3 \times 5 =$ ____

   (a) 8

   (b) 35

   (c) 53

   (d) 15

   (e) We haven't studied this in school yet.

   (f) We've studied this, but it's still hard for me.

14. **How many groups of 2 can you make?**

   (a) 2

   (b) 8

   (c) 9

   (d) 3

   (e) We haven't studied this in school yet.

   (f) We've studied this, but I don't understand it.

15. **Which clock shows 10:30?**

(a)

(b)

(c)

(d)

(e)   We haven't studied this in school yet.
(f)   We've studied this, but it's still hard for me.

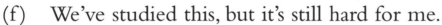
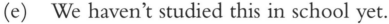

16. **Jane starts practice at 3:00. She practices one half hour. When does she finish?**

(a)   4:00
(b)   3:30
(c)   3:15
(d)   3:00
(e)   We haven't studied this in school yet.
(f)   We've studied this, but it's still hard for me.

17. **How much money is 1 quarter, 1 dime and 1 nickel?**

   (a) 35¢
   (b) 40¢
   (c) 45¢
   (d) 50¢
   (e) We haven't studied this in school yet.
   (f) We've studied this, but it's still hard for me.

18. **Solve the problem. $2.15 + $.89 = ___**

   (a) $3.04
   (b) $2.94
   (c) $2.96
   (d) $3.14
   (e) We haven't studied this in school yet.
   (f) We've studied this, but it's still hard for me.

19. **Which one is less than 1 foot long?**

   (a) a car
   (b) a bed
   (c) a football field
   (d) a crayon
   (e) We haven't studied this in school yet.
   (f)   We've studied this, but it's still hard for me.

20. Find the triangle.

(a) ▢

(b) ▭

(c) ⬠

(d) △

(e) We haven't studied this in school yet.

(f) We've studied this, but it's still hard for me

21. What part of the figure is shaded?

(a) $\dfrac{3}{1}$

(b) $\dfrac{1}{3}$

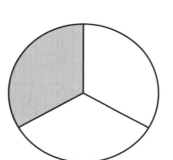

(c) $\dfrac{2}{3}$

(d) $\dfrac{1}{2}$

(e) We haven't studied this in school yet.

(f) We've studied this, but it's still hard for me.

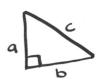

Quiz Me!

Questions 22–23: This graph shows how the kids in second grade voted for their favorite activity. Use it to answer the questions.

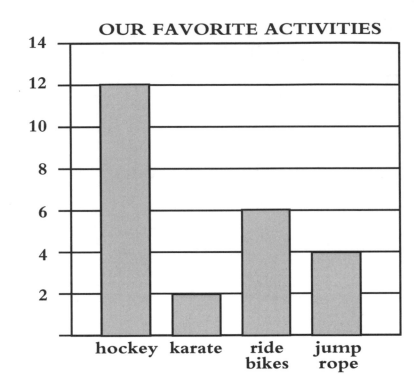

22. Which activity was most popular?

(a) ride bikes

(b) karate

(c) hockey

(d) jump rope

(e) We haven't studied this in school yet.

(f) We've studied this, but it's still hard for me.

23. **How many more children picked hockey than picked jump rope?**

   (a)   3

   (b)   6

   (c)   7

   (d)   8

   (e)   We haven't studied this in school yet.

   (f)   We've studied this, but it's still hard for me.

        ⓐ ⓑ ⓒ ⓓ ⓔ ⓕ

Questions 24–26: Read the problem. Then answer the questions.

Kate got 4 books from the library. She read for 1 hour. Then she played for 2 hours. How long did she read and play?

24. **To answer the question, you must _____.**

   (a)   add

   (b)   subtract

   (c)   multiply

   (d)   divide

   (e)   We haven't studied this in school yet.

   (f)   We've studied this, but it's still hard for me.

        ⓐ ⓑ ⓒ ⓓ ⓔ ⓕ

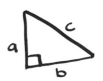

25. **Which information is extra? (You do NOT need it to answer the question.)**

(a)   Kate read for 1 hour.
(b)   Kate played ball for 2 hours.
(c)   Kate got 4 books from the library.
(d)   You need all the information.
(e)   We haven't studied this in school yet.
(f)   We've studied this, but it's still hard for me.

(5,7)

26. **Which sentence will help you solve the problem?**

(a) $4 + 1 + 2 =$ _____
(b) $4 - 2 =$ _____
(c) $1 + 2 =$ _____
(d) $2 - 1 =$ _____
(e)   We haven't studied this in school yet.
(f)   We've studied this, but it's still hard for me.

27. **Which group has only even numbers?**

  (a)   1, 13, 7, 5

  (b)   2, 3, 4, 5

  (c)   10, 8, 6, 4

  (d)   12, 2, 6, 9

  (e)   We haven't studied this in school yet.

  (f)   We've studied this, but it's still hard for me.

  ⓐ   ⓑ   ⓒ   ⓓ   ⓔ   ⓕ

28. **Which numbers equal 16?**

  (a)   5 + 5

  (b)   9 + 7

  (c)   4 + 2

  (d)   5 + 8

  (e)   We haven't studied this in school yet.

  (f)   We've studied this, but it's still hard for me.

  ⓐ   ⓑ   ⓒ   ⓓ   ⓔ   ⓕ

29. **Which numbers equal 5?**

  (a)   12 − 7

  (b)   15 − 9

  (c)   10 − 3

  (d)   3 − 2

  (e)   We haven't studied this in school yet.

  (f)   We've studied this, but it's still hard for me.

  ⓐ   ⓑ   ⓒ   ⓓ   ⓔ   ⓕ

30. **Solve the problem:**

35 + 23 = _____

(a)   85

(b)   12

(c)   56

(d)   58

(e)   We haven't studied this in school yet.

(f)   We've studied this, but it's still hard for me.

31. **Solve the problem:**

57 − 21 = _____

(a)   78

(b)   63

(c)   36

(d)   45

(e)   We haven't studied this in school yet.

(f)   We've studied this, but it's still hard for me.

32. **Which numbers equal 15?**

(a) 5×3

(b) 2×8

(c) 3×6

(d) 2×9

(e) We haven't studied this in school yet.

(f) We've studied this, but it's still hard for me.

33. **What amount do these coins equal?**

(a) 76¢

(b) 37¢

(c) 28¢

(d) 43¢

(e) We haven't studied this in school yet.

(f) We've studied this, but it's still hard for me.

ANSWERS

You're done! Now look up the answers and see how many questions you got right.

1.	c		18.	a
2.	c		19.	d
3.	d		20.	d
4.	d		21.	b
5.	c		22.	c
6.	b		23.	d
7.	d		24.	a
8.	a		25.	c
9.	c		26.	c
10.	c		27.	c
11.	d		28.	b
12.	b		29.	a
13.	d		30.	d
14.	c		31.	c
15.	d		32.	a
16.	b		33.	d
17.	b			

Reading

INTRODUCTION

As you and your child prepare to tackle the questions in this home learning quiz in reading, remember that help is available if you need it. The specific skills tested in this quiz are covered in the companion publication *Learning Adventures: Reading, Grades 1–2,* published by Score@Kaplan and Simon & Schuster. This richly illustrated workbook is full of fun activities that will teach your child all the skills he or she needs to master.

Have your child take each quiz *before* doing the activities in the corresponding workbook, to identify specific areas where she needs more practice. Or have her take the quizzes *after* doing the activities to check on how much she has learned.

Home Learning Quiz

See how many questions you can get right! Follow the directions for each question. Read everything carefully before filling in one answer bubble. Fill in the (e) bubble if you haven't been taught something in the question. Fill in the (f) if you've learned this already in school, but it's still hard for you.

1. **Which set of words is in alphabetical order?**

    (a) doll, book, game
    (b) car, truck, van
    (c) zebra, giraffe, lion
    (d) Juan, Eddie, Tana
    (e) We haven't studied this in school yet.
    (f) We've studied this, but it's still hard for me.

2. **Which letter can be added to the front of the letters *at* to make a real word?**

    (a) z
    (b) d
    (c) h
    (d) j
    (e) We haven't studied this in school yet.
    (f) We've studied this, but it's still hard for me.

3. **Which letter can be added to the back of the letters *an* to make a real word?**

    (a) t
    (b) m
    (c) s
    (d) b
    (e) We haven't studied this in school yet.
    (f) We've studied this, but it's still hard for me.

4. **Which letters are vowels?**

    (a) q, r
    (b) v, x
    (c) o, i
    (d) j, l
    (e) We haven't studied this in school yet.
    (f) We've studied this, but it's still hard for me.

5. **Which word does not have a long vowel sound?**

(a) fish

(b) blue

(c) goat

(d) rain

(e) We haven't studied this in school yet.

(f) We've studied this, but it's still hard for me.

ⓐ ⓑ ⓒ ⓓ ⓔ ⓕ

6. **Which pair of words rhyme?**

(a) tray-tree

(b) chair-seat

(c) tree-me

(d) sun-moon

(e) We haven't studied this in school yet.

(f) We've studied this, but it's still hard for me.

ⓐ ⓑ ⓒ ⓓ ⓔ ⓕ

7. **Which pair of words don't rhyme?**

(a) bear-dare

(b) group-troop

(c) crate-bait

(d) map-mop

(e) We haven't studied this in school yet.

(f) We've studied this, but it's still hard for me.

ⓐ ⓑ ⓒ ⓓ ⓔ ⓕ

8. Which word is not a compound word?

(a) sidewalk

(b) fingernail

(c) running

(d) sunglasses

(e) We haven't studied this in school yet.

(f) We've studied this, but it's still hard for me.

9. Which word has two syllables?

(a) holiday

(b) June

(c) January

(d) Friday

(e) We haven't studied this in school yet.

(f) We've studied this, but it's still hard for me.

10. Which word is plural?

(a) football

(b) shoes

(c) rocket

(d) fire

(e) We haven't studied this in school yet.

(f) We've studied this, but it's still hard for me.

11. The only word that is not plural is _____.

(a) watches

(b) boxes

(c) pencil

(d) toys

(e) We haven't studied this in school yet.

(f) We've studied this, but it's still hard for me.

ⓐ ⓑ ⓒ ⓓ ⓔ ⓕ

12. Which contraction stands for the words *they are*?

(a) they'll

(b) we're

(c) they've

(d) they're

(e) We haven't studied this in school yet.

(f) We've studied this, but it's still hard for me.

ⓐ ⓑ ⓒ ⓓ ⓔ ⓕ

13. Which contraction stands for the words *he will*?

(a) he'll

(b) he's

(c) he'd

(d) we'd

(e) We haven't studied this in school yet.

(f) We've studied this, but it's still hard for me.

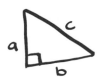

ⓐ ⓑ ⓒ ⓓ ⓔ ⓕ

14. Which name is not the name of a month?

(a) April
(b) October
(c) February
(d) Friday
(e) We haven't studied this in school yet.
(f) We've studied this, but it's still hard for me.

15. Which word can mean a journal, or part of a cut tree?

(a) log
(b) chop
(c) wood
(d) open
(e) We haven't studied this in school yet.
(f) We've studied this, but it's still hard for me.

16. Which word is a synonym for *said*?

(a) spoke

(b) sang

(c) wrote

(d) worked

(e) We haven't studied this in school yet.

(f) We've studied this, but it's still hard for me.

17. Which word is an antonym of *bright*?

(a) shiny

(b) sunny

(c) dull

(d) better

(e) We haven't studied this in school yet.

(f) We've studied this, but it's still hard for me.

18. Which word is a synonym for *thin*?

(a) fat

(b) small

(c) slim

(d) chin

(e) We haven't studied this in school yet.

(f) We've studied this, but it's still hard for me.

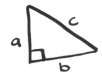

19. Which group of words is a complete sentence?

(a) Del weeded the garden yesterday.
(b) Rode his bike.
(c) My cousin and I.
(d) In the afternoon.
(e) We haven't studied this in school yet.
(f) We've studied this, but it's still hard for me.

20. Which group of words is *not* a complete sentence?

(a) Max mowed the lawn today.
(b) Ate his lunch at 12 o'clock.
(c) Kiernan likes apples a lot.
(d) Apples are good for you.
(e) We haven't studied this in school yet.
(f) We've studied this, but it's still hard for me.

21. **Which sentence should end with a question mark?**

(a) The snow fell softly
(b) What time is it
(c) Gary asked for more milk
(d) It is time to go home
(e) We haven't studied this in school yet.
(f) We've studied this, but it's still hard for me.

ⓐ ⓑ ⓒ ⓓ ⓔ ⓕ

22. **Which sentence usually does *not* end with a question mark?**

(a) Is it 10 o'clock yet?
(b) Jane's dog has spots?
(c) Are you hungry?
(d) How far away is your house from here?
(e) We haven't studied this in school yet.
(f) We've studied this, but it's still hard for me.

ⓐ ⓑ ⓒ ⓓ ⓔ ⓕ

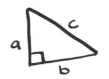

Quiz Me!

23. In which sentence are capital letters used correctly?

(a) Our principal is Mrs. Parsons.
(b) our principal is mrs. parsons.
(c) Our principal is mrs. Parsons.
(d) our principal is Mrs. Parsons.
(e) We haven't studied this in school yet.
(f) We've studied this, but it's still hard for me.

24. Which noun should begin with a capital letter because it is a proper noun?

(a) city
(b) dog
(c) state
(d) ohio
(e) We haven't studied this in school yet.
(f) We've studied this, but it's still hard for me.

30

25. What is the adjective in this sentence?

I love to swim on hot days.

(a) swim

(b) to

(c) I

(d) hot

(e) We haven't studied this in school yet.

(f) We've studied this, but it's still hard for me.

ⓐ ⓑ ⓒ ⓓ ⓔ ⓕ

26. What is the verb in this sentence?

The kangaroo hopped through the trees.

(a) through

(b) kangaroo

(c) hopped

(d) trees

(e) We haven't studied this in school yet.

(f) We've studied this, but it's still hard for me.

ⓐ ⓑ ⓒ ⓓ ⓔ ⓕ

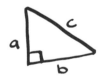

27. Which sentence is correct?

(a) Mom and Dad likes pizza.
(b) Dad and Mom likes pizza.
(c) Mom likes pizza.
(d) Dad like pizza.
(e) We haven't studied this in school yet.
(f) We've studied this, but it's still hard for me.

28. Which verb is in the past tense?

(a) walked
(b) smile
(c) eat
(d) sing
(e) We haven't studied this in school yet.
(f) We've studied this, but it's still hard for me.

29. Which sentence is correct?

(a) They was here yesterday.
(b) We are in Mrs. Johnson's class.
(c) We is sisters.
(d) You is my best friend.
(e) We haven't studied this in school yet.
(f) We've studied this, but it's still hard for me.

30. Which sentence is true about letters?

(a) A letter's closing usually comes just below the date.

(b) The signature is the name of the person you are writing to.

(c) The heading has your address and the date.

(d) A letter's greeting is often Sincerely.

(e) We haven't studied this in school yet.

(f) We've studied this, but it's still hard for me.

31. Which sentence is a description?

(a) The lovely garden has red flowers.

(b) Andy won the race.

(c) Beth sang a song in the talent show.

(d) After the rain, we went out to play.

(e) We haven't studied this in school yet.

(f) We've studied this, but it's still hard for me.

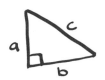

32. A good title for a story about a baseball game is:

(a) Waiting for the Plane
(b) A Home Run for Omar
(c) A Happy Day
(d) Touchdown!
(e) We haven't studied this in school yet.
(f) We've studied this, but it's still hard for me.

33. A story's setting could be:

(a) a girl and her dog
(b) 30 pages
(c) a lost purse
(d) a forest
(e) We haven't studied this in school yet.
(f) We've studied this, but it's still hard for me.

34. **What part of a book gives definitions of hard words from the book?**

(a) Title page

(b) Table of contents

(c) Glossary

(d) Index

(e) We haven't studied this in school yet.

(f) We've studied this, but it's still hard for me.

ⓐ ⓑ ⓒ ⓓ ⓔ ⓕ

35. **Which book is probably a fantasy?**

(a) A Police Officer's Day

(b) Aliens in the Attic

(c) How to Draw Animals

(d) Growing Vegetables

(e) We haven't studied this in school yet.

(f) We've studied this, but it's still hard for me.

ⓐ ⓑ ⓒ ⓓ ⓔ ⓕ

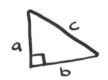

ANSWERS

You're done! Now look up the answers and see how many questions you got right.

1. b
2. c
3. a
4. c
5. a
6. c
7. d
8. c
9. d
10. b
11. c
12. d
13. a
14. d
15. a
16. a
17. c
18. c

19. a
20. b
21. b
22. b
23. a
24. d
25. d
26. c
27. c
28. a
29. b
30. c
31. a
32. b
33. d
34. c
35. b

Science

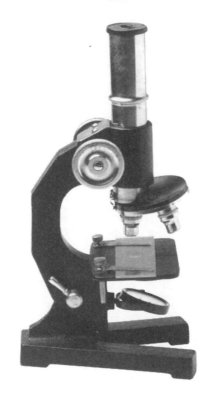

INTRODUCTION

As you and your child prepare to tackle the questions in this home learning quiz in science, remember that help is available if you need it. The specific skills tested in this quiz are covered in the companion publication *Learning Adventures: Science, Grades 1–2,* published by Score@Kaplan and Simon & Schuster. This richly illustrated workbook is full of fun activities that will teach your child all the skills he or she needs to master.

Have your child take each quiz *before* doing the activities in the corresponding workbook, to identify specific areas where she needs more practice. Or have her take the quizzes *after* doing the activities to check on how much she has learned.

Home Learning Quiz

See how many questions you can get right. Read each question before filling in one answer bubble. Fill in the (e) bubble if you haven't been taught something in the question. Fill in the (f) if you've learned this already in school, but it's still hard for you.

1. **How are apples, oranges, and pears alike?**

    (a)   They are all green.

    (b)   They are all yellow.

    (c)   They are all vegetables.

    (d)   They are all fruits.

    (e)   We haven't studied this in school yet.

    (f)   We've studied this, but it's still hard for me.

2. **How are elephants, tigers, and mice alike?**

    (a)   They are all gray.

    (b)   They are all big.

    (c)   They are all heavy.

    (d)   They are all mammals.

    (e)   We haven't studied this in school yet.

    (f)   We've studied this, but it's still hard for me.

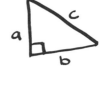

3. **Block** is to *square* as *ball* is to _____.

    (a)   circle
    (b)   square
    (c)   rectangle
    (d)   triangle
    (e)   We haven't studied this in school yet.
    (f)   We've studied this, but it's still hard for me.

4. **Which thing is soft?**

    (a)   tree
    (b)   rock
    (c)   glass
    (d)   fur
    (e)   We haven't studied this in school yet.
    (f)   We've studied this, but it's still hard for me.

5. **Which thing is hard?**

    (a)   jellyfish
    (b)   banana
    (c)   pillow
    (d)   brick
    (e)   We haven't studied this in school yet.
    (f)   We've studied this, but it's still hard for me.

6. Which things belong in the same group?

(a)   dog and baseball

(b)   sand and milk

(c)   apple and rake

(d)   car and bike

(e)   We haven't studied this in school yet.

(f)   We've studied this, but it's still hard for me.

7. Which things _don't_ belong in the same group?

(a)   hockey puck and baseball

(b)   tea and coffee

(c)   orange and corn

(d)   orange and banana

(e)   We haven't studied this in school yet.

(f)   We've studied this, but it's still hard for me.

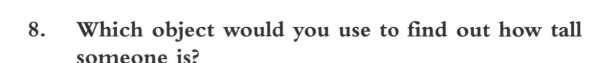

8. Which object would you use to find out how tall someone is?

(a)   balance

(b)   ruler

(c)   shoe

(d)   cubes

(e)   We haven't studied this in school yet.

(f)   We've studied this, but it's still hard for me.

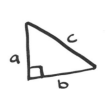

9. **Which object would you use to find out how heavy someone is?**

(a) scale
(b) ruler
(c) measuring cup
(d) microscope
(e) We haven't studied this in school yet.
(f) We've studied this, but it's still hard for me.

10. **What do plants need from the sun to make food?**

(a) roots
(b) light
(c) soil
(d) flowers
(e) We haven't studied this in school yet.
(f) We've studied this, but it's still hard for me.

11. **What part of a plant carries water from the roots to the leaves?**

(a)   seed

(b)   flower

(c)   stem

(d)   leaf

(e)   We haven't studied this in school yet.

(f)   We've studied this, but it's still hard for me.

ⓐ   ⓑ   ⓒ   ⓓ   ⓔ   ⓕ

12. **What do cows eat?**

(a)   grass

(b)   meat

(c)   rocks

(d)   cheese

(e)   We haven't studied this in school yet.

(f)   We've studied this, but it's still hard for me.

ⓐ   ⓑ   ⓒ   ⓓ   ⓔ   ⓕ

13. **What is one way people can help protect Earth?**

(a)   recycle

(b)   cut down trees

(c)   read newspapers

(d)   use paper cups

(e)   We haven't studied this in school yet.

(f)   We've studied this, but it's still hard for me.

ⓐ   ⓑ   ⓒ   ⓓ   ⓔ   ⓕ

14. What thing can you recycle?

(a) newspaper
(b) rotten egg
(c) styrofoam box
(d) dishwashing liquid
(e) We haven't studied this in school yet.
(f) We've studied this, but it's still hard for me.

(5,7)

15. What do seeds need to grow?

(a) air and water
(b) leaves and air
(c) soil and roots
(d) roots and stem
(e) We haven't studied this in school yet.
(f) We've studied this, but it's still hard for me.

16. Which one doesn't melt on a very hot day?

(a) ice cube
(b) ice cream
(c) apple
(d) popsicle
(e) We haven't studied this in school yet.
(f) We've studied this, but it's still hard for me.

17. Which one gives off heat?

(a)   a table

(b)   the sun

(c)   an ice cube

(d)   a shoe

(e)   We haven't studied this in school yet.

(f)   We've studied this, but it's still hard for me.

18. Which one can be a solid, a liquid, or a gas?

(a)   water

(b)   air

(c)   sock

(d)   sponge

(e)   We haven't studied this in school yet.

(f)   We've studied this, but it's still hard for me.

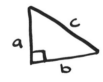

19. To make a shadow larger, what should you do?

(a)   Move the object closer to the light.

(b)   Keep the object in one place.

(c)   Move the object farther away from the light.

(d)   Turn the light off.

(e)   We haven't studied this in school yet.

(f)   We've studied this, but it's still hard for me.

20. **What object can a magnet lift?**

   (a)   a crayon
   (b)   a button
   (c)   a paper clip
   (d)   a book
   (e)   We haven't studied this in school yet.
   (f)   We've studied this, but it's still hard for me.

21. **During which season are you most likely to see leaves falling from trees?**

   (a)   winter
   (b)   spring
   (c)   summer
   (d)   fall
   (e)   We haven't studied this in school yet.
   (f)   We've studied this, but it's still hard for me.

22. **During which season are you most likely to turn on your air conditioner?**

    (a)　winter
    (b)　spring
    (c)　summer
    (d)　fall
    (e)　We haven't studied this in school yet.
    (f)　We've studied this, but it's still hard for me.

23. **There are cumulus clouds in the sky and it is very hot. What kind of weather will there most likely be?**

    (a)　rain
    (b)　fair weather
    (c)　snow
    (d)　hail
    (e)　We haven't studied this in school yet.
    (f)　We've studied this, but it's still hard for me.

24. **The weather is sunny, and there are thin, high clouds in the sky. What kind of clouds are those?**

(a) cumulus
(b) cirrus
(c) stratus
(d) nimbus
(e) We haven't studied this in school yet.
(f) We've studied this, but it's still hard for me.

25. **Where does the water in clouds come from?**

(a) the sun
(b) the planets
(c) the sky
(d) oceans, streams, lakes, and rivers
(e) We haven't studied this in school yet.
(f) We've studied this, but it's still hard for me.

26. **What causes day and night?**

(a) the movement of the planets around the sun
(b) the movement of the earth around the sun
(c) the movement of the sun around the earth
(d) the movement of the moon around the earth
(e) We haven't studied this in school yet.
(f) We've studied this, but it's still hard for me.

27. What do the planets move around?

(a)   Earth
(b)   Sun
(c)   Moon
(d)   other stars
(e)   We haven't studied this in school yet.
(f)   We've studied this, but it's still hard for me.

28. Which planet has living things on it?

(a)   Mars
(b)   Earth
(c)   Moon
(d)   Jupiter
(e)   We haven't studied this in school yet.
(f)   We've studied this, but it's still hard for me.

29. Which is closest to Earth?

(a)   Sun
(b)   Moon
(c)   Neptune
(d)   Mars
(e)   We haven't studied this in school yet.
(f)   We've studied this, but it's still hard for me.

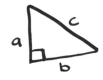

30. **The remains of animals or plants that lived long ago are called _____.**

(a)   dinosaurs

(b)   rocks

(c)   fossils

(d)   sand

(e)   We haven't studied this in school yet.

(f)   We've studied this, but it's still hard for me.

31. **Which dinosaur is the biggest?**

(a)   brontosaurus

(b)   tyrannosaurus rex

(c)   pterodactyl

(d)   ankylosaurus

(e)   We haven't studied this in school yet.

(f)   We've studied this, but it's still hard for me.

32. **Which dinosaur can fly?**

(a)   brontosaurus

(b)   tyrannosaurus rex

(c)   pterodactyl

(d)   ankylosaurus

(e)   We haven't studied this in school yet.

(f)   We've studied this, but it's still hard for me.

33. Which animal and plant live in the ocean?

(a) squirrel and seaweed
(b) fish and pine tree
(c) crab and coral
(d) bird and raspberry bush
(e) We haven't studied this in school yet.
(f) We've studied this, but it's still hard for me.

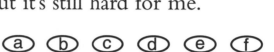

34. Which animal can swim in water and hop on land?

(a) whale
(b) frog
(c) dolphin
(d) chicken
(e) We haven't studied this in school yet.
(f) We've studied this, but it's still hard for me.

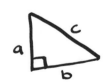

35. **You are in the air traveling from one part of the country to another. What are you traveling in?**

    (a)   a car

    (b)   an airplane

    (c)   a motorcycle

    (d)   a train

    (e)   We haven't studied this in school yet.

    (f)   We've studied this, but it's still hard for me.

36. **Which way of traveling is slowest?**

    (a)   by car

    (b)   by airplane

    (c)   by motorcycle

    (d)   by horse

    (e)   We haven't studied this in school yet.

    (f)   We've studied this, but it's still hard for me.

37. **Which foods would be found in a healthy diet?**

(a) chocolate, cake, and corn
(b) broccoli, banana, and cotton candy
(c) fish, rice, and apple
(d) hamburgers, french fries, and soda
(e) We haven't studied this in school yet.
(f) We've studied this, but it's still hard for me.

38. **Which foods would *not* be found in a healthy diet?**

(a) ice cream, cookies, and butter
(b) milk, fish, and rice
(c) apple, chicken, and milk
(d) banana, broccoli, and bread
(e) We haven't studied this in school yet.
(f) We've studied this, but it's still hard for me.

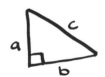

ANSWERS

You're done! Now look up the answers and see how many questions you got right.

1.	d		20.	c
2.	d		21.	d
3.	a		22.	c
4.	d		23.	a
5.	d		24.	b
6.	d		25.	d
7.	c		26.	b
8.	b		27.	b
9.	a		28.	b
10.	b		29.	b
11.	c		30.	c
12.	a		31.	a
13.	a		32.	c
14.	a		33.	c
15.	a		34.	b
16.	c		35.	b
17.	b		36.	d
18.	a		37.	c
19.	a		38.	a

Animals

INTRODUCTION

As you and your child prepare to tackle the questions in this home learning quiz, remember that help is available if you need it. The specific math, reading, and science skills tested in this quiz are covered in the companion publication ***Learning Adventures: Animals, Grades 1–2,*** published by Score@Kaplan and Simon & Schuster. This richly illustrated workbook is full of fun activities that will teach your child all the skills he or she needs to master.

Have your child take each quiz *before* doing the activities in the corresponding workbook, to identify specific areas where she needs more practice. Or have her take the quizzes *after* doing the activities to check on how much she has learned.

Home Learning Quiz

See how many of these you can get right! Read carefully. Use scrap paper if you need to write anything down. Then fill in the answer bubble. Fill in the (e) bubble if you haven't been taught something in the question. Fill in the (f) bubble if you've learned this in school, but it's still hard for you.

1. **Choose the meaning for the underlined word that fits in the sentence.**

    The buzzing <u>bug</u> kept me awake.

    (a)   a mistake in a computer program
    (b)   a minor illness or germ
    (c)   an insect
    (d)   to bother
    (e)   We haven't studied this in school yet.
    (f)   We've studied this, but it's still hard for me.

ⓐ ⓑ ⓒ ⓓ ⓔ ⓕ

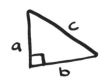

2. **Choose the meaning for the underlined word that fits in the sentence.**

We were having so much fun, time just seemed to <u>fly</u> by.

(a)   a baseball that has been hit high into the Air
(b)   a winged insect
(c)   to move through the air
(d)   to pass quickly
(e)   We haven't studied this in school yet.
(f)   We've studied this, but it's still hard for me.

Questions 3–4: *Answer the questions about this sentence:*

An elephant is a <u>big</u> animal.

3. **Which word is a synonym for the underlined word?**

(a)   tiny
(b)   huge
(c)   old
(d)   silly
(e)   We haven't studied this in school yet.
(f)   We've studied this, but it's still hard for me.

4. Which word is an antonym for the underlined word?

(a) chubby
(b) gray
(c) enormous
(d) small
(e) We haven't studied this in school yet.
(f) We've studied this, but it's still hard for me.

5. What is an antonym for the underlined word in the sentence below?

The <u>noisy</u> seals at the zoo barked at each other all day.

(a) quiet
(b) loud
(c) fat
(d) ugly
(e) We haven't studied this in school yet.
(f) We've studied this, but it's still hard for me.

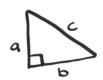

6. **Which is an example of a compound word?**

(a) fishing

(b) goldfish

(c) gold ring

(d) golden

(e) We haven't studied this in school yet.

(f) We've studied this, but it's still hard for me.

7. **Which group has three rhyming words?**

(a) true, new, do

(b) grow, cow, slow

(c) ran, rain, run

(d) crash, bath, watch

(e) We haven't studied this in school yet.

(f) We've studied this, but it's still hard for me.

8. **Which group does *not* have three rhyming words?**

(a)   true, new, do

(b)   grow, cow, slow

(c)   rain, grain, lane

(d)   late, weight, rate

(e)   We haven't studied this in school yet.

(f)   We've studied this, but it's still hard for me.

9. **Which sentence shows alliteration?**

(a)   I saw a few turtles.

(b)   A turtle carries its own shell.

(c)   Turtles take too much time.

(d)   A turtle is a reptile.

(e)   We haven't studied this in school yet.

(f)   We've studied this, but it's still hard for me.

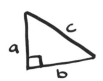

10. Select the best title for the story.

At first, a baby frog doesn't look like a frog. When it hatches from its egg, it looks like a fish. Soon it grows legs. Then the tail drops off. Finally, the baby looks like a little frog.

- (a) "Ribbit!" Said the Frog
- (b) Baby Frogs Change
- (c) Frogs Can Hop
- (d) Frogs Come from Eggs
- (e) We haven't studied this in school yet.
- (f) We've studied this, but it's still hard for me.

11. Which word is the action verb in the sentence below?

Bats fly at night.

- (a) bats
- (b) fly
- (c) at
- (d) night
- (e) We haven't studied this in school yet.
- (f) We've studied this, but it's still hard for me.

12. The contraction for *they would* is _____.

    (a)   they'd
    (b)   we're
    (c)   aren't
    (d)   they've
    (e)   We haven't studied this in school yet.
    (f)   We've studied this, but it's still hard for me.

ⓐ ⓑ ⓒ ⓓ ⓔ ⓕ

13. Which group of words is in alphabetical order?

    (a)   zebra, yak, quail
    (b)   parrot, hamster, dog
    (c)   ant, pig, hippo
    (d)   camel, horse, robin
    (e)   We haven't studied this in school yet.
    (f)   We've studied this, but it's still hard for me.

ⓐ ⓑ ⓒ ⓓ ⓔ ⓕ

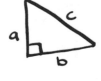

14. Which word pair includes only living things?

    (a)   pencil, flower
    (b)   rock, table
    (c)   dog, doll
    (d)   tree, kangaroo
    (e)   We haven't studied this in school yet.
    (f)   We've studied this, but it's still hard for me.

ⓐ ⓑ ⓒ ⓓ ⓔ ⓕ

15. Which sense does the sentence tell about?

The girl stroked the chinchilla's soft fur.

(a)   touch
(b)   smell
(c)   sight
(d)   hearing
(e)   We haven't studied this in school yet.
(f)   We've studied this, but it's still hard for me.

16. Which animal is not a mammal?

(a)   elephant
(b)   goldfish
(c)   human
(d)   cat
(e)   We haven't studied this in school yet.
(f)   We've studied this, but it's still hard for me.

17. Which animal is not a fish?

(a) seal

(b) salmon

(c) shark

(d) trout

(e) We haven't studied this in school yet.

(f) We've studied this, but it's still hard for me.

18. What is the name for a group of wolves?

(a) pride

(b) school

(c) pack

(d) bed

(e) We haven't studied this in school yet.

(f) We've studied this, but it's still hard for me.

19. What is the name for a baby bear?

(a) pup

(b) fawn

(c) cub

(d) kitten

(e) We haven't studied this in school yet.

(f) We've studied this, but it's still hard for me.

Quiz Me!

20. **Which animal's habitat is the desert?**

    (a)   rattlesnake

    (b)   whale

    (c)   cow

    (d)   penguin

    (e)   We haven't studied this in school yet.

    (f)   We've studied this, but it's still hard for me.

21. **What are you most likely to see near your house?**

    (a)   forks, dinosaurs, and sand

    (b)   boats, sharks, and redwood trees

    (c)   birds, flowers, and children

    (d)   cars, tigers, and mountains

    (e)   We haven't studied this in school yet.

    (f)   We've studied this, but it's still hard for me.

22. Where would you find cactus and a coyote?

    (a)   rain forest

    (b)   desert

    (c)   forest

    (d)   ocean

    (e)   We haven't studied this in school yet.

    (f)   We've studied this, but it's still hard for me.

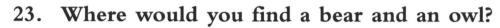

23. Where would you find a bear and an owl?

    (a)   rain forest

    (b)   desert

    (c)   forest

    (d)   ocean

    (e)   We haven't studied this in school yet.

    (f)   We've studied this, but it's still hard for me.

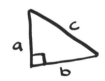

24. Which group would you find in an ocean?

    (a)   beaver, seal, oak tree

    (b)   frog, spider, eel

    (c)   coral, blue whale, octopus

    (d)   squirrel, octopus, monkey

    (e)   We haven't studied this in school yet.

    (f)   We've studied this, but it's still hard for me.

25. Which animal is a mammal?

    (a)   snake

    (b)   bird

    (c)   dog

    (d)   lizard

    (e)   We haven't studied this in school yet.

    (f)   We've studied this, but it's still hard for me.

26. What do birds have that no other animals have?

    (a)   wings and feathers

    (b)   ears and eyes

    (c)   paws and tails

    (d)   fur and beaks

    (e)   We haven't studied this in school yet.

    (f)   We've studied this, but it's still hard for me.

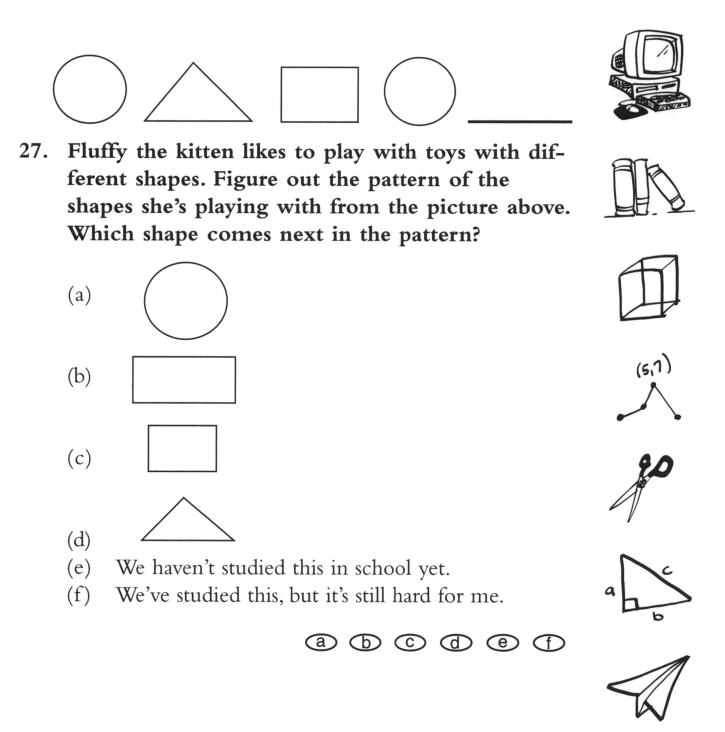

27. **Fluffy the kitten likes to play with toys with different shapes. Figure out the pattern of the shapes she's playing with from the picture above. Which shape comes next in the pattern?**

(a)

(b)

(c)

(d)

(e)   We haven't studied this in school yet.

(f)   We've studied this, but it's still hard for me.

ⓐ ⓑ ⓒ ⓓ ⓔ ⓕ

Quiz Me!

28. Barney the dog stole $\frac{1}{2}$ of the pizza that the Dobson family was planning to eat for dinner. Which picture shows how much he ate?

(a)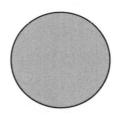

(b)

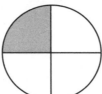

(c)

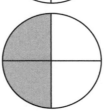

(d)

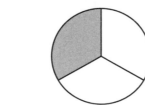

(e) We haven't studied this in school yet.
(f) We've studied this, but it's still hard for me.

29. Which statement is true?

(a)   6 rabbits < 4 rabbits

(b)   9 rabbits > 7 rabbits

(c)   3 rabbits < 2 rabbits

(d)   1 rabbit > 5 rabbits

(e)   We haven't studied this in school yet.

(f)   We've studied this, but it's still hard for me.

ⓐ ⓑ ⓒ ⓓ ⓔ ⓕ

30. What do all reptiles have?

(a)   wings

(b)   fur

(c)   feathers

(d)   scales

(e)   We haven't studied this in school yet.

(f)   We've studied this, but it's still hard for me.

ⓐ ⓑ ⓒ ⓓ ⓔ ⓕ

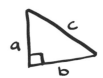

ANSWERS

You're done! Now look up the answers and see how many questions you got right.

1.	c		16.	b
2.	d		17.	a
3.	b		18.	c
4.	d		19.	c
5.	a		20.	a
6.	b		21.	c
7.	a		22.	b
8.	b		23.	c
9.	c		24.	c
10.	b		25.	c
11.	b		26.	a
12.	a		27.	d
13.	d		28.	c
14.	d		29.	b
15.	a		30.	d

How Do You Foster Your Child's Interest in Learning?

In preparing this series, we surveyed scores of parents on this key question. Here are some of the best suggestions:

- Take weekly trips to the library to take out books, and attend special library events.

- Have lots of books around the house, especially on topics of specific interest to children.

- Read out loud nightly.

- Take turns reading to each other.

- Subscribe to age-appropriate magazines.

- Point out articles of interest in the newspaper or a magazine.

- Tell each other stories.

- Encourage children to write journal entries and short stories.

- Ask them to write letters and make cards for special occasions.

- Discuss all the things you do together.

- Limit TV time.

- Provide educational board games.

- Keep the learning experiences fun for children.

- Watch selected programs on TV together, like learning/educational channels.

- Provide project workbooks purchased at teacher supply stores.

- Take trips to museums and museum classes.

- Supply lots of arts and crafts materials and encourage children to be creative.

- Visits cities of historical interest.

- Encourage children to express themselves in a variety of ways.

- Take science and nature walks.

- Teach children to play challenging games such as chess.

- Supply lots of educational and recreational computer games.

- Discuss what children are learning and doing on a daily basis.

- Visit the aquarium and zoo.

- Cook, bake, and measure ingredients.

- Encourage children to participate in sports.

- Listen to music, attend concerts, and encourage children to take music lessons.

- Be positive about books, trips, and other daily experiences.

- Take family walks.

- Let children be part of the family decision-making process.

- Give a lot of praise and positive reinforcement for your child's efforts.

- Review child's homework that has been returned by the teacher.

- Encourage children to use resources such as the dictionary, encyclopedia, thesaurus, and atlas.

- Plant a vegetable garden outdoors or in pots in your kitchen.

- Make each child in your family feel he or she is special.

- Sit down together to eat and talk.

- Don't allow children to give up, especially when it comes to learning and dealing with challenges.

- Instill a love of language; it will expose your child to a richer thought bank.

- Tell your children stories that share, not necessarily teach a lesson.

- Communicate your personal processes with your children.

- Don't talk about what your child did not do. Put more interest on what your child did do. Accept where your child is at, and praise his or her efforts.

- Express an interest in children's activities and schoolwork.

- Limit TV viewing time at home and foster good viewing habits.

- Work on enlarging children's vocabulary.

- Emphasize learning accomplishments, no matter how small.

- Go at their own pace; People learn at different rates.

- Challenge children to take risks.

- Encourage them to do their best, not be the best.